MIKE ANGELL

How Can I Live Peacefully with Justice?

CHURCH PUBLISHING INCORPORATED

A little book of guidance

Copyright © 2020 by Mike Angell

All rights reserved. No part of this book may be reproduced, stored in a retrieval system, or transmitted in any form or by any means, electronic or mechanical, including photocopying, recording, or otherwise, without the written permission of the publisher.

Unless otherwise noted, the scripture quotations are from New Revised Standard Version Bible, copyright © 1989 National Council of the Churches of Christ in the United States of America. Used by permission. All rights reserved worldwide.

Church Publishing
19 East 34th Street
New York, NY 10016
www.churchpublishing.org

Cover design by Jennifer Kopec, 2 Pug Design
Typeset by Denise Hoff

A record of this book is available from the Library of Congress.

ISBN-13: 9781640652101 (pbk.)
ISBN-13: 9781640652118 (ebook)

Printed in Canada

*Dedicated to all the folks
with whom I have marched
(in church or the streets)
and especially to Ellis and Silas.*

Contents

1. *What Do We Mean by Peace?* — 1
2. *If We Don't Get No Justice . . .* — 11
3. *Building Peace Locally: Laundry and Guns* — 15
4. *Building Peace Internationally: El Salvador* — 31
5. *Building Peace with Myself* — 43

Epilogue — 57

1 ▪ *What Do We Mean by Peace?*

It may seem odd that a priest from one of America's most violent cities has been asked to write a book of guidance about peace. The image of St. Louis around the world has been reshaped in recent years. I moved to St. Louis, Missouri, seven months before Michael Brown was killed by a police officer in Ferguson. The story of Michael's death, the protests, the media attention, the questions raised are well-known. It would be impossible to write about peace from Missouri without reflecting on the events of August 2014 and what they revealed about our city, our nation, our world.

I chose that word "revealed" carefully. Michael's death and the protests surrounding it seemed to surprise the world. In parts of my community, Michael's death was experienced not as an anomaly, but as an uncovering. This is a violent city. In 2017 the *Guardian* newspaper named a stretch of Natural Bridge Avenue, just a few miles from where Michael died, the center of America's gun violence epidemic. Of course, yard signs in St. Louis proclaim "Black Lives Matter," but on the city's north side, another sign is even more common. It reads: "We Must Stop Killing Each Other." St. Louisans know we have a problem with violence. In the months that followed August 2014, the world would learn about a specific violent dynamic at play in our streets.

What was uncovered in the streets, on social media, and over live television was the dynamic of fear that exists between Black residents and the police. This fear wasn't new. This fear was generational. In the months that followed, the deaths of Tamir Rice in Cleveland, Freddie Gray in Baltimore, Sandra Bland in Texas, and others revealed that the fear wasn't just local. Black parents fear that their children will be killed by an officer of the peace.

What was different about August of 2014, and what has been different in my city since that month, is an unwillingness to "return to normal." Black activists, young people who gathered in the streets of Ferguson, refused to quiet down, refused to back down. As my Methodist colleague the Rev. Willis Johnson has said, it was as though a "slowly dripping dam had broke open."[1] Those leaders would not allow the city to return to police business as usual. Protests continued for over 100 days and nights. The activists wouldn't allow the old game of covering up injustice to continue.

I watched the refusal to allow a cover-up play out in St. Louis's streets from a particular vantage point as a Christian in the "Episcopal branch of the Jesus Movement" (as our presiding bishop likes to say). Every Sunday the first prayer a priest prays, at the front of the congregation gathered for Eucharist, is the Collect for Purity: "Almighty God, to you all hearts are open, all desires known, and from you no secrets are hid. . . ."[2] Christians believe in a God who is in the business of uncovering, revealing, exposing. At the very beginning of our service every Sunday, we acknowledge our vulnerability. Before God no secrets are hidden, no desires are unknown, and no hearts are closed.

The prayer book knows there can be no peace without vulnerability. We live in a world that pretends the opposite. We equate

---

1 Willis Johnson, *Holding Up Your Corner* (Nashville, TN: Abingdon Press, 2017), xv–xvi.

2 The Episcopal Church, *The Book of Common Prayer* (New York: Church Publishing, 1979), 355.

peace with a lack of conflict. Our tax structures are built to maximize the resources for policing in response to violence. More than half of our taxes in St. Louis go to support public safety.[3] If our police officers have the latest equipment, if our local police force carries military grade weaponry, we tell ourselves, they can keep the peace. The Ferguson uprising uncovered a wide separation between the culture of police departments and the people who are policed.

Ferguson also taught us that the police were the vanguard of a deeper enforced separation. The Ferguson uprising uncovered the deeply persistent segregation. We are taught to hope, to dream, to pray separately. So how could a pastor who works so close to Ferguson write a book about peace? I would argue that we won't know peace unless we are willing to face uncovering. Ferguson showed us how much we have relied on a false peace. Real peace doesn't come from a show of force. Real peace is not one-sided. Real peace requires that my neighbor have peace. Peace requires revelation. We have to be willing to be vulnerable. We have to be willing to move with God to a place where we know our neighbors' fears. We must know what keeps folks up at night. We must know what our most vulnerable communities count as injustice. Until we know what causes our neighbors' nightmares, can we honestly say we know how to dream of a godly peace? Are we willing to work, with God, for a peace in which no secrets are hid?

Living with peace means being willing to become uncomfortably vulnerable, and working for justice requires building unlikely

---

3 Expenditure Data, St. Louis, MO.gov, accessed May 19, 2020, https://www.stlouis-mo.gov/government/departments/budget/transparency/expenditure/index.cfm.

relationships of trust. Living with peace also means knowing ourselves. Finding real peace means facing elements of our own stories that are painful to confront. We all, all of us, need to work to reconcile our own sense of self, our own identity, if we are ever to be able to reconcile with others. Peace only exists in relationship.

The Role of the Church in Peacemaking

Scripture—especially the writings of the New Testament—can serve as a resourceful companion for Christians living in these difficult days. As Phyllis Tickle, Brian McLaren, and many others have written, we are facing a turning point for the church in North America and Western Europe. "Christendom" is coming to an end, the scholars tell us. Shrinking Sunday attendance is the primary data. For the first time since the early centuries of the Christian movement, Christians may not be the gatekeepers of power. Christians may find themselves on the margins. Aren't the margins exactly where the followers of Jesus belong?

It is hard not to greet the news as a loss. But, in the counterintuitive logic of faith, loss can also be gain. Christianity's marriage to power also meant that the faith was used to justify the structures of that power. Christianity was used to bless a particular constellation of identities: whiteness, maleness, European, heterosexual, land-owning, able-bodied, etc. Losing an attachment to patriarchal, homophobic, racist, ableist, xenophobic power structures could bring us back to the heart of Christianity. Losing our marriage to unjust power might indeed take us back to our roots as followers of a first-century Palestinian Jew.

What Do We Mean by Peace?

If the scholars are right, we are beginning to know something like the reality of the early disciples. The Gospels, the Epistles, all the writings of the New Testament were written by a people who counted as outsiders. The peace that Jesus proclaimed stood in contrast to the officially proclaimed *Pax Romana*, the supposed peace of Rome. Jesus and his followers witnessed to a different kind of peace.

As Christians this moment may represent a chance to go back to our roots, to be known as the Church was in the early centuries, as a movement engaged with the disenfranchised. The Romans mocked the Jesus movement as a religion for women and slaves. If our movement knows those on the receiving end of injustice, Christianity can be a resource for folks who seek justice, who question the status quo. But asking these questions is difficult: because asking questions about power, asking questions about structural change, requires a willingness to question relationships with the current power structures.

I moved to St. Louis from Washington, DC. I had served a parish in the heart of our nation's capital, and at the heart of our idea of a Christian nation: St. John's, Lafayette Square sits across from the White House. President Madison wanted a church close to the president's base of operations. Every president since Madison has attended services there. Bright yellow St. John's, the church of the presidents, is one of the most vivid symbols of my denomination's historically close relationship with the power structures of our society.

That closeness comes with both difficulty and responsibility. Asking questions of justice can be difficult when you are close to power. Upsetting the status quo might jeopardize budgets and buildings. But proximity to power also means that sometimes our church has the capacity to focus attention. We have the ability to influence the conversation about the meaning of peace.

What Is Peace?

What is peace? What do we mean by the word? When we slow down and ask the question, the answer can become surprisingly difficult. We might think of peace in the way our nation's founders thought of the truths of human rights. We might think of peace as "self-evident." We know peace when we see it, when we feel it.

But the meaning of peace can be fearfully contextual. What one group in society experiences as the dream of peace, another may experience as a nightmare. In the suburbs of Denver, where I grew up, the police are often called "officers of the peace." But a few miles from where I live now, on Canfield Drive in Ferguson, Missouri, Black parents worry about police officers as dangerous. Parents teach their children to keep their hands in full view around police, teach them to say "yes, sir" and to answer questions politely. When protests erupted after Michael Brown's death, municipal leaders called for "peace." But chants echoed from the streets in response, "if we don't get no justice, then you don't get no peace." The word "peace" can have a contested definition.

Jesus makes a distinction. "Peace I leave with you; my peace I give to you. I do not give as the world gives. Do not let your hearts be troubled" (John 14:27). The world in the time of Jesus claimed to be at peace. But the *Pax Romana*, the so-called peace of Rome, was a violent and fearful reality for Jesus's people. Rome's "peace" relied on the repression of the people of Galilee, Palestine, all the

Roman colonies. The Roman armies were funded by the taxes of the colonized. Those without Roman citizenship knew terror. Their hearts were troubled. They lived in fear of uniformed officers of the Roman regime. They lived with anxiety, that their neighbors might be collaborating with the empire. In the midst of this so-called "peace," Jesus preached a different sort of peace.

In Matthew's Gospel, Jesus tells the disciples, "Do not think that I have come to bring peace to the earth; I have not come to bring peace, but a sword" (Matt. 10:34). Jesus then tells his followers he will set father against son, mother against daughter. Jesus divides the family quicker than a discussion of the current presidency at the dinner table. "Do not think I have come to bring peace," Jesus says, at least not the kind of peace you know.

The Southern poet William Percy penned perhaps the most artful distillation I know of Jesus's definition of peace. One of his poems is included in the 1982 Hymnal as Hymn 661: "They Cast Their Nets in Galilee." The poem tells of the call of the disciples, and the final stanza measures the cost of following Jesus:

> The peace of God, it is no peace
> But strife closed in the sod.
> Yet let us pray for but one thing —
> The marvelous peace of God![4]

Percy describes peace theologically. Peace is a gift, but it is also a challenge. Christ's peace is costly. The "marvelous peace of God" requires a willingness to engage in conflict, a willingness to know the ways our neighbor's hearts are troubled. God's peace requires

---

[4] Episcopal Church. 1985. The Hymnal, 1982: service music : according to the use of the Episcopal Church. New York: Church Hymnal Corp.

we become willing to uncover the strife buried just beneath the topsoil. Peace requires the courage to stir up the status quo. God's peace is relational. God's peace demands work to uncover hidden injustice. We witnessed an uncovering in the streets of Ferguson, and in conversations between neighbors discussing Ferguson. Working for equitable peace is disruptive. That disruption will be met with practiced opposition by those the unjust systems benefit.

When we talk about peace, too often we speak in the negative. Peace, we assume, is the absence of violence. We also describe peace as the absence of other things: of noise, of distraction, of conflict. We are all looking for a little peace and quiet. Such negative descriptions of peace ask us to carve small islands in our calendars and in our cities. We talk about "peaceful neighborhoods." We create "peaceful places" = libraries, churches. We look for peaceful time as well. I defend the twenty minutes in the morning after my husband, Ellis, has departed and our son, Silas, is dropped at daycare, before my commute begins. In an overbusy and hectic culture, such spaces and pauses are important, for sure. But we treat peace like a resource we can protect.

That we treat peace as a resource helps to explain why this definition of peace does not play well across divisions of class and race. In the years since Michael Brown's shooting, I have heard the chant I mentioned earlier again and again in the streets of my city. "If we don't get no justice, then you don't get no peace." Peace in the negative, peace as an island of comfort and quiet, is a luxury in this city. Not everyone can afford the luxury of peace.

Peace described in the negative also protects the status quo. City leaders in St. Louis have called for peace each time folks have taken to the streets. "If the protestors would just settle down, if ministers would stop asking questions, criticizing police, if we could all just go back to the way things were, we could have peace." I have heard similar pleas again and again from folks who look like me. Since moving to St. Louis, I have heard friends and family members, many of whom grew up in majority white suburbs like Golden, Colorado, where I grew up, wish that the protests would just "settle down." "We just want peace," they say. I have learned to question that understanding of peace.

Learning from the Modern Saints: Dr. King

Martin Luther King Jr. knew peace and quiet did not necessarily go hand in hand. In a lecture occasioned by his accepting the Nobel Peace Prize, Dr. King said, "We will not build a peaceful world by following a negative path."[5] He knew firsthand what it was to be told to settle down, to keep the peace. Brother Martin was made a saint in the Episcopal Church. He has been given a feast day, which can be a dangerous thing to do to a leader. Today's civil rights activists worry that Dr. King's legacy has been sanitized by textbooks and politicians who quote his gentler words. We forget how radical his voice sounded in his own day.

Schoolchildren memorize quotes from Dr. King's "Letter from a Birmingham Jail." White preachers quote him from the pulpit and forget to whom the letter was addressed. King's letter from jail was a response to another missive. A group of clergy leaders, including two Episcopal bishops from Alabama, wrote to him first.

---

5 The Rev. Dr. Martin Luther King. "Nobel Lecture." 11 Dec. 1964 https://www.nobelprize.org/prizes/peace/1964/king/lecture/

How Can I Live Peacefully with Justice?

They sought to persuade the civil rights leader to leave their state. They asked him, as an outsider, to stay away. Leaders of my own denomination signed a letter asking Dr. King to let Alabama take its own time. In response, he wrote that the greatest stumbling block to the work for civil rights was not the Klu Klux Klan but

> the white moderate, who is more devoted to "order" than to justice; who prefers a negative peace which is the absence of tension to a positive peace which is the presence of justice; who constantly says: "I agree with you in the goal you seek, but I cannot agree with your methods of direct action"; who paternalistically believes he can set the timetable for another man's freedom.[6]

Like Jesus, Dr. King made a distinction about peace. He refused to define peace negatively. He steadfastly refused calls from civic leaders, from his fellow clergy, to allow the civil unrest to quiet down. Dr. King wasn't looking for quiet. He was looking for change. He was looking for justice. Dr. King knew his dream could not be achieved unless the nightmares of segregation and violent oppression were addressed. He was done waiting. He was going to turn over the soil and plant seeds of a peace the world was not able to give.

---

[6] The Rev. Dr. Martin Luther King. "Letter from Birmingham Jail." 16 Apr. 1963 https://www.africa.upenn.edu/Articles_Gen/Letter_Birmingham.html

2 ▪ If We Don't Get No Justice . . .

I first heard the name Michael Brown from the pulpit of Christ Church Cathedral the day after he was killed. The Very Rev. Mike Kinman told the congregation he had to throw out his original sermon the night before, after he had heard about the young man who had been shot by a police officer. Michael Brown's body had been left in the street for five hours in the hot August sun. Rumor had it that Michael's hands were up in surrender when he was shot.

That morning, the news of a young Black man killed by a police officer struck me as an unusual reason to rewrite a sermon. Black men were killed by police officers with frequency. (I hadn't yet registered the problematic nature of my own surprise.) As I heard Dean Kinman preach, as I heard the anger in his voice, I didn't yet know that his anger reflected the emotion in the streets. The dean had lived in St. Louis much longer than I. He was a priest with deep roots in the community. Before he rewrote his sermon, Kinman went up to Ferguson and gathered with the young activists who were planning action in response to Michael Brown's death.

I mentioned parenthetically my surprise at the sermon. I want to pause a moment in that surprise. By the time I moved to St. Louis, I thought of myself as reasonably aware of dynamics around race and power. As you'll read in a later section, I had done work around listening to the fears of my friends who were Black. The thing about unconscious bias is that it is unconscious; it requires uncovering. My in-built assumptions about policing and power were going to be challenged.

How Can I Live Peacefully with Justice?

Until I heard Dean Kinman's sermon on that hot August morning, until I had gone with my fellow clergy to "pray with our feet," as the Rev. Traci Blackmon said of our first march, I didn't really understand the systemic dynamic. I knew intellectually that more people of color were incarcerated. I knew the courts often failed to hold folks accountable for racial violence. But I grew up with the assumption that you could trust police officers. My limited interactions with the police before Ferguson had reinforced my impression, that the police were folks who chose a career to serve and protect. I was initially surprised that my neighbors could not make similar assumptions. I discovered I could make two responses to my surprise: I could resist the new information, and explain that I had only known good and kind police officers, or I could listen to my neighbors and believe their fear was credible.

For many of those first months my new Midwestern city felt sleepy, especially after the relentless news cycles of Washington. The sleepiness obviously didn't last. At the time, I was working on the staff of the presiding bishop of the Episcopal Church as Missioner for Young Adult and Campus Ministries. Dean Kinman had also invited me to serve as a volunteer priest associate at the St. Louis Cathedral. August 10 was a Sunday when I did not have duties to preach or to celebrate, which is why I sat in the pew with my spouse to hear the dean's angry rewrite, to hear him reflect the discontent growing in the streets of Ferguson. Later that week, I traveled with the Cathedral clergy just a few miles up the highway to my first protest in my new city.

National news reporters I recognized from Washington started showing up in Ferguson. As I had done in the capital, I found myself asking, "What does it mean to do ministry at the center

If We Don't Get No Justice . . .

of the nation's attention?" I figured, like in most ministry, you start by showing up. I accepted the invitations of colleagues, lay and ordained, to come to Ferguson to pray and to march. I wasn't the only one. People started turning up from around the country to march in the streets of my new city.

"If we don't get no justice, then you don't get no peace." I had heard the chant in protests in other cities. Before I came to St. Louis, I had marched with young Black activists in Washington after the killing of Trayvon Martin, and again after the acquittal of his killer. But I had never heard as many voices shouting the words. I had never heard the words chanted with such conviction, such a sense that the stakes were so immediate. Something changed in Ferguson. Something was uncovered. The words were spoken with new urgency.

I've preached sermons about the poetic possibilities I find in this chant. The shortened version of "If we don't get no justice, then you don't get no peace" is simply "No justice; no peace." I have said from the pulpit, more than once, that when I hear the words, "No justice; no peace," I imagine an alternate spelling: "Know justice; know peace." The threat becomes a prescription. "If you want peace, work for justice"[7]—those words from Pope Paul VI were quoted often in my undergraduate courses on theology. I became used to making my own translation for the chant. I was comfortable with my role as a preacher. I knew how to spiritualize protest.

My translation got harder in the streets of Ferguson. My role as a clergyperson, as a person of faith, was more difficult as well.

---

7 Pope Paul VI, "If You Want Peace, Work for Justice," Vatican, January 1, 1972, http://www.vatican.va/content/paul-vi/en/messages/peace/documents/hf_p-vi_mes_19711208_v-world-day-for-peace.html.

How Can I Live Peacefully with Justice?

Leaders in Ferguson added a third line to the chant: "No justice, no peace." The well-known words were followed with, "No racist police." No justice, no peace, no racist police. I couldn't reframe that last bit as easily. I had to learn to question my long-held assumptions. The words spoke to the intransigence of generational injustice. If we want to know peace, to really know peace, the work won't be easy. It isn't a simple trick of the language. Real justice requires engaging systemic injustice, even questioning systems we have learned to trust. Working for peace, real peace, isn't fast. Peace requires an undoing of the status quo. Peace means dismantling systems that keep some people safe at the expense of others.

3 ■ *Building Peace Locally: Laundry and Guns*

Laundry Love

The parish I now serve, Holy Communion in University City, Missouri, does a lot of laundry. Most months, I join church members at our Laundry Love ministry. Those two hours I spend talking with neighbors, building Legos, or helping kids with homework, and trying to be somewhat useful as folks get their laundry done are usually the best two hours of my month. Sometimes I pray with someone who has lost a job, is facing surgery, or is worried about a grandchild. Sometimes I have to mediate an argument over a line for washers. Still, I usually end the night saying, "This is why I think church matters."

Managing a church, like running any nonprofit or business, can be stressful. Sundays come with certain pressures. Everyone wants a little bit of the pastor's time. There are too many requests to remember. Sometimes the checklists required for leading others in prayer distract from my ability to pray. I spend a good bit of energy on Sundays wondering if the sermon landed the way I hoped, or trying to remember which people I saw in the line after the service I wanted to e-mail or call to follow up. But the Tuesday nights I spend at Laundry Love provide my most reliable glimpse of the kind of transformational peace I believe Jesus envisioned.

The Road to Laundry Love

I met my congregation on the streets of Ferguson. At the time, as I said, I was working on the staff of the presiding bishop. I wasn't really looking for a job, though I was missing day-to-day ministry with folks in a local church. Holy Communion surprised me from the get-go. I had come to my first protest on Florissant Avenue, led by the Rev. Traci Blackmon. There were a lot of clergy, but only one Episcopal congregation showed up with a number of lay folk. What struck me was the diversity: Black women in their seventies and white teenagers marching side by side.

I was under instruction from my supervisors in the presiding bishop's office: "Don't get arrested unless the bishop of Missouri is getting arrested." My activism could apparently cause political problems within the wider church. So I walked the streets of Ferguson during that first protest with Bishop Wayne Smith of Missouri and I asked him, "What congregation is that with such a diverse group of folks marching?" He didn't answer my question directly. He simply said, "Oh, they're looking for a rector. You should apply." I told him I wasn't looking for a job. He encouraged me to give their parish profile a look.

We got started with the laundry about a year after I started as rector. When I first came to the church, the leadership was looking for an outreach ministry of their own. We helped run a food pantry and Sunday lunch program at another parish in another part of town. We had several members who were involved in important work for justice and equity outside of church life, but Holy Communion didn't have an outreach ministry that felt like ours, that we held sole responsibility to cultivate and manage. We decided to start simply. We decided to try laundry.

Building Peace Locally: Laundry and Guns

A small team gathered to talk through a new ministry startup. The "Laundry Love" concept wasn't ours originally. We had watched videos[8] and heard news stories[9] about churches in California taking over laundromats one night a month and simply paying for anyone's laundry who showed up. The volunteers turned a laundromat into a community center for a night. The stories we heard about Laundry Love were filled with laughter and smiles between neighbors. It seemed like something we could manage, and Laundry Love looked fun.

We started planning. For six months we scouted out locations. We met at laundromats and washed our own clothes. While the washers and dryers tumbled and spun, we talked through our hopes for the ministry. We read materials from the Laundry Love organization.[10] We talked strategy. Three people stepped up to head up the ministry and rotate the lead role of assigning volunteers, as well as ensuring we had soap and quarters and all the other necessary items.

After six months of meeting, we were ready for a pilot. We settled on a little family-owned laundromat just a few blocks from the church. The owner was happy to host us and earn a little extra income on a slow night of the week. But more than that, he was happy we wanted to help folks who were struggling just to get their clothes washed. The small business had been running for

---

8 "Laundry Love," The Episcopal Church, July 3, 2014, https://episcopalchurch.org/library/video/laundry-love.
9 "A Growing Movement to Spread Faith, Love—And Clean Laundry," NPR, July 27, 2014, https://www.npr.org/2014/07/27/335290086/a-growing-movement-to-spread-faith-love-and-clean-laundry.
10 Laundry Love: https://laundrylove.org/get-involved/.

decades. The owner knew a lot of people around the neighborhood were making hard financial decisions. He was glad for a partnership with a church in helping. Partnership helped the ministry succeed.

We decided to spend two months doing a "soft open." We wanted to have room for reflection before and after each event before we opened the doors wide to new volunteers. We did some limited advertising about the nights: flyers at the local library, word of mouth in nearby food pantries. We determined the third Tuesday of each month would be the evening, closer to the end of the month when checks and food stamps start to run low and folks have to make harder financial decisions. The volunteer team met half an hour before the loads began. We set up our posters, set out pizza, and checked in with the staff of the laundromat. We set up a kids' activity area where students could get homework help and little ones could color or play while their parents or caregivers did the laundry.

Those first two months helped us to iron out the wrinkles. We decided we needed to advertise "kids' activities" rather than "free babysitting," after a parent wanted to drop the kids off and leave the building. We figured out a system for signing in and assigning tickets to ensure the first who came were the first to load their clothes in the machines. We tried to make check-in feel more like a restaurant with a greeter at the door taking names, instead of asking people to stand in a long line. The greeters lent a sense of dignity, and made sure guests were welcomed with a smile. The first two months allowed us to identify problems, but when we gathered to talk after each of the first two nights, the overall feeling among the volunteers was gratitude. To a person, we'd had a great time. We'd met neighbors we didn't know we had. We'd shared stories and laughter.

From the get-go, Laundry Love felt like a ministry that fit Holy Communion. Early in my time at the church, I asked the congregation to reflect as we sought to write a new mission statement and to set goals together. I'd settled on three simple questions that got folks storytelling:

- What brought you to Holy Communion?
- What keeps you at Holy Communion?
- In five years, what do you want your neighbors to know about Holy Communion?

People talked a lot about the sense of welcome they felt in the parish, an uncommon sense that folks at the church wanted to know you and make you feel at home. Parishioners talked about their love of a congregation the reflected the diversity of the neighborhood, the same diversity that originally caused me to ask the bishop about the congregation. They talked about the community that existed within the walls of the church and the community they wanted to serve outside their walls.

Holy Communion, I learned, had moved to this inner suburb from the center city. In 1938, the downtown neighborhood where the original church stood was emptying of congregants. Holy Communion became a "white flight" church, following white members who left as Black people moved into the original neighborhood. But thirty years later, when the neighborhood around the new church started to change, the congregation made a different choice. Holy Communion performed the first interracial marriage in the diocese. And the parish was one of the first in the state of Missouri to integrate, in the 1960s.

Holy Communion sits on Delmar Avenue, the road that has been the historic dividing line segregating St. Louis. The church is on the north side of the street, the side where African Americans have historically lived. In University City, the area around the church, the segregation line was often drawn a little farther north, but geography still tells a story. Holy Communion's location on the north side of that psychological line mattered. Some of the first Black families that joined Holy Communion were also the first families to integrate white neighborhoods in our municipality. For sixty years the church has been a bridge-builder.

Laundry Love felt like a right next step for the congregation, particularly at a laundromat so close to the church. Seeing the diversity of the volunteers from Holy Communion made folks visiting Laundry Love curious. There aren't many churches where people worship together across lines of race and class. The ministry also broadened our horizon as a congregation. Laundry Love introduced us to neighbors living within walking distance of the church who are struggling to make ends meet, folks who weren't knocking on the doors of the church.

Almost three years into Laundry Love, there are nights when it is hard to tell who is a volunteer, who is a guest, and who has just dropped in to say, "Hi." Sometimes some of our regulars will come by the laundromat on Laundry Love night, even without clothes to wash or a volunteer job. They simply want to catch up with neighbors, or check in on a friend.

Part of the beauty of this model of ministry is the lack of serving tables. Volunteers don't stand on one side with guests on the

Building Peace Locally: Laundry and Guns

other. There aren't firm divides between those who are serving and those who are being served. For a lot of the night, after the clothes and quarters are in the machine, there's nothing to do but stand around and talk. We laugh as someone tries to contain the bubbles spilling out of a machine that got too much soap. We hear old stories from the neighborhood and the latest gossip about University City politics. We ask how kids are doing in school.

At Laundry Love, I pretty regularly get asked about our church. One night I met a middle-aged Black woman. For the sake of privacy, I'll call her Aisha. My husband, Ellis, introduced us. Aisha heard that the quarters were coming from a church, and so she asked Ellis, "What does your church believe?" Ellis didn't quite know how to answer, so he introduced her to me, the priest. I'd had a few encounters in the laundromat where folks asked what we believe. The question always made me a bit nervous.

Many of those who come to Laundry Love attend churches with firm answers and less mystery than our tradition. Having been quizzed before by members of other denominations who wanted to know if we were a legitimate Christian group, I started into a conversation with Aisha about the Trinity and the Nicene Creed. I even tried to narrate a bit about the English Reformation.

She glazed over at my response. She wasn't interested in my explanation that Episcopalians weren't heavy on doctrine, or my lesson about history. Luckily Gretchen, a longtime member of our church and also a Black woman, was listening in. She asked what we were talking about. I said, "Aisha wanted to know what we believe." Gretchen didn't let me finish my overwrought answer. Instead she jumped in,

How Can I Live Peacefully with Justice?

"At Holy Communion, we believe in love, in respect, in dignity, in community, diversity, and welcome."

Aisha beamed. "I can believe in that. When are your services?"

What if we all learned to talk about our faith like Gretchen? What if we worried less about the contours of doctrine and more about the depth of wisdom our faith has offered us? What if we worried less about the formal vocabulary, the theology, the orthodoxy of it all? What if we offered space for prayer, for empathy, for love, and to work for justice? What if that is how we described our journey together first, by our common commitments and the wisdom we have gained?

For all the time we had spent together at church, I realized I didn't know Gretchen was so articulate about why church mattered to her. Laundry Love has given us the opportunity to spend time together in new ways. This ministry of soap and quarters has asked us to simply show up, and has given us time to talk with neighbors we had otherwise been kept from meeting. Laundry Love builds relationships that would be unlikely to occur in our city.

Jesus told us that the greatest commandment was to love God and then to love our neighbors. Laundry Love has helped move those neighbors from a theoretical idea to a concrete set of faces. Many of the folks who come to the laundromat will never join our church, but that's not the point. We've built relationships, and we've come to better know the struggles going on around us.

Yes, we can measure success in numbers. We keep careful tab on the total amount of money spent (usually a few thousand dollars a year: you can only spend so much on laundry machines in a given set of hours). We tally the number of loads completed. But the relational benefits are often greater than the numbers can measure. We've helped introduce a neighbor who was living in an apartment with toxic mold and an absentee landlord to a free legal clinic. She was rehoused in a clean comfortable senior apartment. One of our ministry leaders, through the local PTA, got information for Laundry Love included in every back-to-school packet our district sent out last year. We've connected a couple of folks to job training programs.

Yes, Holy Communion is a "diverse church" as Episcopal churches go, but nuances in balance matter. We have more than the average share of people of color in our pews, but we are still majority white. The people of color in our congregation are just as likely to have an advanced degree and an important title as the white folks. We've learned through laundry love that part of what we have to share is social capital. We have relationships that can help open a door, secure an interview, make sure a city official follows up. Laundry Love hasn't yet righted a great injustice in the city, but the relationships built have helped to bring about change in a few lives.

I have come to think of Laundry Love sacramentally. Those Tuesday nights, once a month, point to a deeper reality. Though we are divided by lines of segregation based on race, income, or education, we can find common ground. We can build community. We can learn to stand together in a way that doesn't privilege just a few of us. I've been surprised by the way God has showed me the difference that can be made simply by knowing your neighbors.

The peace I find at Laundry Love lasts for just a few hours a month, but glimpses matter. If we are to build peace with justice, I'm convinced it will happen faster if neighbors who have been kept from knowing one another have a chance to meet. Peace, with justice, is the product of turning over the tables that usually stand between the servers and those who are served. Real peace happens when we stand together, we laugh, we cry, we pray, we conspire. Real peace happens when we just stand around and listen to one another.

I have come to rely on Laundry Love the way I rely on Eucharist. I live in a city that is painfully divided. Laundry Love gives me a glimpse that another peace is possible.

Gun Violence

St. Louis has been called the epicenter of America's gun violence epidemic. The city ranks higher than any other in the United States for shootings per capita. The Very Rev. Kathie Adams-Shephard succeeded Mike Kinman as dean of Christ Church Cathedral. Each Sunday she places one candle on the high altar for every person killed with a gun in St. Louis. This past November, as we met in the Cathedral to elect our next bishop, 178 candles flickered, reminding the delegates at convention of the ongoing epidemic of gun violence, reminding us of each life lost in our city.

Holding a candle in a dark church has been marked some of the most memorable moments in my religious upbringing. I loved services when the church got out the little plastic candleholders. We only got to use them at the most special moments of the church year, Christmas and Easter. When we got out the little handheld candles, you knew church was getting serious. As a kid holding that candle, I would try to make patterns with the dripping wax on the candleholder, or the bulletin.

Building Peace Locally: Laundry and Guns

The first time I saw one of those candleholders outside church, a shooting had just occurred at a neighboring high school. Growing up in Jefferson County, Colorado, I attended a college-prep option school. Several of my classmates from elementary, who didn't attend the option school, were students at Columbine. I'll never forget the afternoon of April 20, 1999, and the image of an assistant principal rushing up the sidewalk by the school's temporary buildings where my English class was held. He burst into our classroom and whispered in the teacher's ear before locking the door on his way out.

We were "on lockdown" for several hours. Eventually we were allowed to exit our classroom, go back into the main building, and call our parents. The busses took us home and we didn't return for more than a week. In the days that followed, students from around the county attended a number of memorial services and vigils. I went to at least three hosted by megachurches my friends attended. We wore blue and silver ribbons, said prayers, and held candles. Those same candles I knew from Easter and Christmas took on a new layer of meaning.

I was lucky. No one I knew died at Columbine. But I also had a sense life wouldn't be the same. My parents used to talk about the moment they heard that Dr. King was killed, or JFK. Columbine would be that moment for me, I thought. Now, when I see those candles at Christmas and Easter, they are accompanied by memories of high school friends with tears, and new fears of guns.

Today I can't count the number of times I have held a candle after a mass murder. Columbine, Virginia Tech, Charleston, Las Vegas, the Tree of Life synagogue, the New Zealand mosque shooting, and the Pulse Nightclub all come to mind quickly, but I've been to more. The candles are a pretty steady fixture.

When my mother was in seminary, it became a bit of a joke in our house to say, "Light a candle for me" whenever she had a big test or an interview with a committee voting on her ordination. "I have a test in my Hebrew Bible class," she'd say, "light a candle for me." While the request was a joke in our house, her request had an appealing practicality. Often when we ask folks for their prayers, it feels so intangible. Lighting a candle was something we could actually do. At least one of the times she asked, I went into a church, put a quarter in the slot of one of those ancient wrought-iron candle stands with the red votive glass candleholders, and lit a candle.

In prayer, prepositions matter. While lighting a candle FOR someone feels practical, lighting a candle WITH someone means something else entirely. I mentioned in my list of mass shooting vigils the Pulse nightclub. When a gunman attacked a gay nightclub in Orlando on June 12, 2016, the terror hit close to home in a way I hadn't felt since Columbine. I spent several nights when I was in my twenties dancing in clubs like Pulse. I remember the freedom I felt the first time I walked into a packed gay club, the sense that the space was safe for me in a way I hadn't known before.

"Straight" bars and clubs always made me nervous. I often entered these spaces with women friends. I watched as the men in the bar watched my friends, and then sized me up. I worried if it became obvious that I was gay that I might be perceived as an obstacle. I worried if they took an interest in my friend and that interest wasn't reciprocal, that I might be blamed. I didn't like the spaces generally. The combination of patriarchal culture and alcohol is dangerous. A lot of queer folk get threatened in "straight" spaces. Walking into a gay club, that pressure was off. I had a sense of safety.

At 2:00 a.m. on Sunday, June 12, a gunman killed forty-nine queer folk and wounded fifty-three others at the Pulse nightclub in Orlando. Less than twenty-four hours later and half a country away, St. Louis marched. We have gotten good at marching. A crowd of around twelve hundred gathered in "The Grove," the hub of gay nightlife in the city. We chanted as we made our way to the Transgender Memorial Garden, a scrubby patch of ground kept by local activists in memory of far too many transfolk who have been killed or who have died by suicide in our city.

At the vigil's destination, a few speakers haphazardly took the stage. The organizers obviously hadn't planned for such a large gathering. Organizers led more chants, and eventually some songs. It was almost impossible to hear from where I stood. But they had asked everyone to bring their own candles. I borrowed some from the Easter and Christmas stockpile at church.

Standing in that park as an early summer sunset turned the sky orange and seeing candles light the diverse faces of the queer community, we sang to fill the silence: "This little light of mine, I'm gonna let it shine." I didn't know how much I needed to stand with people, to sing, and to feel the presence of others who were similarly terrified. I had attended so many vigils since my first as a sixteen-year-old kid. I stood FOR people whose names I knew from the news. Lighting a candle WITH my fellow queer folks that night made a difference. I didn't know there would be a hymn among the chants. "This Little Light of Mine" will now carry the dual meaning of the candles for me. The hymn has taken on new meaning and a sense of solidarity because of the memories of the vigil.

How Can I Live Peacefully with Justice?

I debated, but I wore my collar that night. I needed the night personally, but I also needed to link that march to my faith and my faith community's work on gun violence. A number of people from our church also marched and sang. Some came because they too needed to be with their fellow LGBTQ+ folks. Others came out of solidarity.

Our congregation has been pushing for sensible gun reform in Missouri. We regularly write our state senators and our US senators. We've gathered signatures and marched. After the shooting in Parkland, we brought one of the largest contingents to the St. Louis "March for Our Lives." Our congregation has written postcards and signed online petitions after Sunday worship. We've called and organized. Still, Missouri's legislature has worked to loosen restrictions and make it easier to carry a gun.

Among the marchers that night in The Grove was a mother from our congregation. She lost her son to gun violence before I was called to Holy Communion as a priest. Like me, many of the white parishioners can point to particular shootings that "hit close to home." Many of my Black parishioners talk more relationally, naming a sibling, a child, a cousin, a best friend who was shot. These aren't easy stories to tell. They don't often make the front page. Shootings in the Black community often don't even make the news. Last year in St. Louis over a dozen children were killed by guns. All of them were Black.[11]

---

11 "Coverage of Children Who Died in the St. Louis Area in 2019," *St. Louis Post-Dispatch*, December 30, 2019, https://www.stltoday.com/news/local/crime-and-courts/coverage-of-children-who-died-in-the-st-louis-area-in-2019/collection_e4c6a022-f048-59df-9a40-cd54c0173f34.html#31.

Building Peace Locally: Laundry and Guns

I have a colleague who became a priest after retiring from a career in hospital administration. The Rev. Marc Smith started a grant-funded program to study whether we can curb gun violence by supporting victims of gun violence and their families who arrive at the hospitals. Giving those who have been affected by gun violence access to social workers, mental healthcare, and job training is showing some promising results. The highest indicator that someone will commit a gun crime is whether they have had a gun crime committed against them. Marc is now regularly invited to pray at meetings of local gun control advocates. When legislative victory for sensible gun reform feels so impossible in our state, it helps to feel we can make progress outside the political debates.

In recent years we formed a group at the parish, "Faithful Action." Ninety or so of our members are on an e-mail list and text chain. We invite one another to sign petitions, to register voters, to call our legislators. The Faithful Action group were the principle members who joined us in The Grove on the night of the Pulse vigil. A few of us are working to build a wider organization of churches in the St. Louis region that could act together.

Dean Kathie Adams-Shepherd of Christ Church Cathedral keeps lighting candles. Every year on the first of January she starts the count again. She told me recently that at the start of the year lighting the candles only takes a few minutes. By the end of the year, it takes almost an hour. She and a few members of the 8 a.m. congregation at the Cathedral light the candles together. Three of those early service members have taken it upon themselves to clean the candleholders, to boil off the spent wax, and prepare the glass for the next week's services.

How Can I Live Peacefully with Justice?

Dean Kathie started the practice of lighting candles after the shooting in Parkland, but she had been engaged in prayer and activism around gun violence for a number of years. I first met her at a protest in Washington, DC. She came because at the time she was the rector of the Episcopal church in Newtown, Connecticut. After the traumatic shooting in Newtown, and her pastoral response, she was invited by a group of bishops to help lead prayers for change in Washington. I had gotten involved in the small Episcopal protest the week before Holy Week because I was already in Washington, and because of my own history growing up so near Columbine. Because of her connection to Newtown, Dean Kathie often is asked to be interviewed by local reporters when a shooting reaches the national news.

As she lit candles for the students who died in Florida, Dean Kathie told me she asked, "And how many people have died in St. Louis this year?" After Parkland, she decided to restart the high-altar vigil, but to number local victims. The candles became a way to pray, but she says, they are also a reminder. They are a reminder to the congregation that prayer sometimes isn't a private activity. They are a reminder that most victims of gun violence aren't killed in mass shootings that grab headlines. They are a reminder to make phone calls to local legislators. They are a reminder to write letters to politicians and letters to the editor. The candles are a reminder to keep showing up. In Missouri, it can be easy to just throw up your hands when it comes to the question of guns. The political deck seems impossibly stacked. Sometimes the work of the church is not letting the candle go out.

4 ▪ *Building Peace Internationally: El Salvador*

Learning from Modern Saints: The Land of Romero

"Isn't El Salvador dangerous?"

I'm asked a version of that question almost every time I take a trip to the country. I started visiting regularly before seminary, when I was on the staff of the Episcopal Diocese in San Diego. Over a number of years, the country and the people wove their way into the fabric of my faith. When I became rector of Holy Communion, I asked members of the congregation to go with me. Soon afterward, our vestry voted to establish a relationship with a human rights organization, Cristosal, based in El Salvador. Three years into the relationship, and fifteen years after I first started leading groups, people still ask if it's safe.

The question, from one perspective, is fair. El Salvador has one of the highest per capita murder rates in the world. This perception is carried pretty heavily in the media. Hardly a story is written in the English-speaking press covering El Salvador for anything other than violent gangs. Since I live in St. Louis, I have a pretty quick response, "Yes, El Salvador has a high murder rate, but the city of St. Louis actually has a higher rate of gun violence, so statistically you are safer in El Salvador than if you stayed home. You want to come along?"

Perspective matters. It is easy to dismiss a country or a neighborhood as "unsafe," to say that the homegrown violence makes working there unwise. It is harder to ask questions about why certain places are allowed to be violent and others are safeguarded as peaceful.

I've even been asked in Spanish if I knew how violent El Salvador was. The first time I "met" El Salvador (in Spanish the word *conocer* is used to describe meeting a person or encountering a whole nation), I took a bus from the country next door. I was living on the campus of a foster-care facility in Tegucigalpa, the capital of Honduras, while I served for a year after college with the Episcopal Church's Young Adult Service Corps. A number of my Honduran hosts were concerned when I shared my travel plans.

"Are you sure you want to go there? El Salvador is very dangerous," they warned. El Salvador's reputation is bad even in Central America (though Honduras has a similar rate of violence). My friend Cheryl reassured me. She said we'd be safe—and anyway she had already purchased tickets for the bus.

Cheryl came down to visit Honduras during our winter break. After seeing where I was serving, she wanted to show me the country where she had spent a few months as a volunteer. We boarded the bus and rode into El Salvador. Over three days we visited the beach town where Cheryl had spent the previous summer. We hiked in a hillside park near San Salvador, and climbed a rock formation known as the Devil's Door, with impressive views over the capital city, a volcano, and the Pacific. I tried my first Salvadoran *pupusa*, a delicious stuffed corn tortilla grilled to order. The Salvadorans were welcoming. They were willing to talk about their recent history of violence, and tell stories about their local saint.

Meeting Cheryl's host family was great, but it was the chance to see the martyred Archbishop Oscar Romero's country that made

Building Peace Internationally: El Salvador

me to agree to the trip. That first visit, for me, was a pilgrimage. The archbishop lived the message of liberation theology, the commitment of God to the well-being of the poor and persecuted. He had become a guiding saint. I wanted to walk a little closer to his footsteps.

Romero was chosen as archbishop from among El Salvador's bishops in 1977, at a time of great conflict in the country over potential land reform. Rural farmworkers, *campesinos*, were demanding a larger share of the proceeds of their labor. The handful of families that owned the majority of the land resisted. Rome thought Romero was a quiet bookworm who wouldn't make trouble for the church in the growing conflict.

Early in his time as archbishop, a close friend of Romero's, a Jesuit priest named Rutilio Grande, was killed because he was ministering with people seeking freedom from poverty. Grande's murder forced Romero to come out more publicly for reform. Sometimes liberation theology is dismissed as "spiritualized communism," but Grande and Romero were no communists. They were suspicious of Marx's denial of God and his emphasis on human agency. Still, they saw in the struggle of the poor the call of Jesus to care for the "least of these." They encouraged small groups to gather to study the Bible. Much of the now famous liberation theology grew out of these small Bible studies, known as "base communities." As regular Salvadorans read the Gospels, they had the sense that the salvation Jesus promised had practical implications in their lives. They asked why so much wealth was concentrated in so few hands, when so many of God's people went hungry.

Even before his public pronouncements on wealth and poverty, Romero chose a simple life for such a grand appointment. When he was named archbishop, Romero did not accept the fancy residence offered to the church by a wealthy family. Instead he set up a cot in the sacristy behind the chapel of a small cancer hospital. The nuns who ran the hospital eventually had a three-room house built for the him on the grounds. When they went to give him the keys, they decided to ask the cancer patients to walk the archbishop to his little private residence. The sisters say they knew Romero wouldn't turn down a gift from the patients.

Even after he moved into the house, some mornings the nuns still found him asleep back in the sacristy. The archbishop confessed he had been scared by the sound of mangos falling onto the tin roof of his little home, afraid that someone had lobbed a grenade over the compound's wall to kill him. His choice to stand with the poor carried heavy consequences. The death threats he received frightened him. He had reason to fear.

It was in that hospital chapel where Romero was murdered. The Sunday before he had preached a barnstormer of a sermon. Romero's homilies were broadcast across the country on Catholic radio. He regularly preached a vision of the peace that could be possible if the army would stop meeting calls for justice with violence. He described Jesus's vision of the kingdom of God as a real way of relating to one another across divides of ethnicity and economic class.

Romero's final Sunday sermon reached a height of political critique, blasting the world being built by the Salvadoran regime on the backs of rural farmworkers. From the pulpit of the cathedral he commanded the army "cease the repression." A few nights after his sermon, the archbishop was once again in church. One of the nuns had asked him to say mass for a family member who had died.

As he prepared the altar, an off-duty army officer pulled up on the street in front of the chapel, took aim, and ended Romero's life.

The blood-stained vestments Romero wore the night of his murder, along with his glasses, and his worn-out old rosary are on display in his little house on the hospital grounds. Over the years I have been visiting, the nuns have steadily converted the rooms into a small museum. They display his day-to-day life: his slippers, his typewriter, his tape recorder. The archbishop's little two-door Corona is still parked outside; the Toyota manual is on his bookshelf.

The way the archbishop chose to live was itself a protest. Archbishops tend to circulate among a country's elite. Romero wanted to be with the people who most needed him. I remember walking through the display on that first trip, I was struck how common the saint's stuff made him seem. Here was a regular human being, unassuming, just making it through life. Photos of him laughing with friends, towels, a hammock in the corner, his toothbrush, all of it fit in three little rooms.

There is a certain peace on the grounds of the little hospital. All around the traffic of San Salvador churns. Though a number of pilgrims arrive each day to visit the museum, to pray in the chapel, and to remember Romero, the voices are hushed. The cancer hospital itself isn't a museum. Advanced cancer patients still fill the wards, attended by the sisters. The hospital accepts folks regardless of their ability to pay. The wealthy and the poor spend their last days together. The Rt. Rev. Martín Barahona, retired Anglican bishop of El Salvador, was a patient there before his death in 2019. Martín said it was a privilege to spend his last days so close to Romero.

Bishop Barahona had met with the archbishop before he converted to Anglicanism, back when he was a young Catholic priest. Even after he became an Anglican, he counted Romero as one of his personal saints. Barahona had to flee his country for a number of years after Romero's death. The civil war that followed the assassination claimed almost seventy-five thousand lives. Half a million were internally displaced and had to move from their homes into makeshift camps in safer zones of the country, driven away by death threats. Another half million became refugees to neighboring countries and the United States. Martín spent much of the war serving as a priest in Panama. He was elected bishop of El Salvador the year the peace accords that ended the war were signed. Bishop Barahona worked to shape the Salvadoran Anglican Church into a force for justice. He founded the nonprofit with which our parish now partners: Cristosal.

Cristosal: Human Rights and Peacemaking

"How do you feel about participating in a prophetic revolution?" The question from Noah Bullock was more practical than what I was studying in seminary at the time. In the years I'd known him, Noah had never been one to waste much time with small talk. But this one was even more direct. Noah wasn't thinking about the idea of revolution. He was building one.

Noah and I both moved to Central America to work with the Episcopal Church in 2005, but we didn't meet until a couple of years later. I went home after my volunteer year in Honduras was up. Noah stayed on in El Salvador. When I was back stateside, my bishop tapped me to help lead trips to our partner diocese in El Salvador, because I "had experience in Central America."

Building Peace Internationally: El Salvador

I had accepted a job working to replant a campus ministry at the University of California, San Diego. Since I was on the bishop of San Diego's staff, the relationship with El Salvador became one of my "other duties as assigned." I was grateful for the assignment. Noah was my local contact. Over much of the next decade and a half, Noah and I have worked together each time I brought a group to El Salvador. We have gotten to know one another pretty well over the visits, and now meet up in the United States as well. When he asked me about the revolution, it was because Bishop Barahona had just asked him to take over as director of Cristosal.

The more time I spent with Noah, the more I was taken aback by the degree of his immersion in Salvadoran culture and politics. I thought I spoke Spanish well, but Noah swears like a local. When I first met him, Noah lived in a house provided by the diocese in the country's Southeastern province, but he often spent nights in a hammock in El Carmen or Canoa, small impoverished towns where he worked.

Watching Noah on one particular April "Alternative Spring Break," a trip I made with a collection of college students recruited from the campus ministry, I remembered my time in Tegucigalpa. Living in Honduras and slowly learning a language was tough for me. The culture shock was ongoing, and so whenever a group came from the States, I rushed to meet the North Americans. I hungered for those visits, the chance to talk with people who spoke my language literally and culturally. Noah did the opposite.

I noticed that Noah dutifully spoke with the college students from San Diego and answered their questions. But when we arrived in a community, Noah was quick to jump from the truck to catch up on the local news. He chatted with the leaders of the community, asking about their latest dealings with the mayor over water rights; he checked in on a woman who'd been having a rough time with a pregnancy. For Noah, driving around our group of visitors was an excuse to go and spend time with his Salvadoran friends.

One day our group had worked hard on the service project and was asleep in the back of the van. Noah and I were free to talk to each other. He was fascinated by my decision to go to seminary. We had both grown up sons of Episcopal priests, intimately close to the institutional church, but he couldn't identify with my desire to be ordained. Noah often claimed to be unsure about his own faith.

"I just don't know about religion," he said. He explained that he believed in a higher power, but had big doubts about Church. Why did Jesus need to be more than a social revolutionary?

On that long car ride, we debated, of all things, the merits of transubstantiation. Noah was hung up on this idea: why did the Church need to believe that through some sort of ancient hocus-pocus bread and wine became God's flesh and blood? It seemed to him both incredible and incredibly unnecessary. In those days, in addition to the development work, Noah's position with the diocese required that he spend Sundays helping a local priest. They traveled together from community to community. I thought of Noah, gathered with the townspeople under an ad hoc canopy of dried palm leaves, watching as the priest lifted up the bread and the cup. Noah wasn't sure that the bread and wine were mystically changed, but he did believe the people deserved real transformation.

I kept visiting, kept leading trips. And Cristosal started shifting. Noah's "prophetic revolution" was slow but steady. Noah and his coworkers eventually incorporated Cristosal separately from the diocese. They wanted the organization to be more than the "social projects" arm of the church. Cristosal focused on building awareness of human rights, and the capacity for local advocacy. Instead of arriving with a truck full of bricks to build a clinic or a bridge, Cristosal arrives with community organizers and attorneys. They help communities access and influence their local governments.

Cristosal also has a different vision for the work of North Americans who come to visit El Salvador. Traditional "mission trips" travel to build churches, housing, clinics, schools, or wells. The Cristosal Global School was founded to teach a human rights and advocacy curriculum. North American tuitions help fund stipends for Central Americans to join in the courses, and an international group learns together from local advocates and leaders. The courses often begin with Noah offering an introduction to human rights.

Noah says he is reticent to talk about God, but in these seminars he sounds like a religion professor. He asks, "Where do human rights come from?" Then he leads the group in a discussion about how human beings are "endowed by their Creator" with "certain unalienable rights." He talks about human rights as a framework that transcends international borders and the claims of individual religions. For Cristosal, this framework of rights is truly universal.

The first time The Episcopal Church of the Holy Communion came with me to see Cristosal's work, we travelled to a neighborhood outside San Salvador. We saw a local success story. Organizers from Cristosal had been offering training and support to a community of women who were pushing back on patterns of violence. Their neighborhood was perceived within the country as extremely dangerous. A few of the Salvadoran participants in our Global School class were visibly nervous as we made our way into the cinder block community center.

After a couple of hours of shared activities, conversations about how our various communities were affected by violence, the women took us on a tour of their neighborhood. We were accompanied by a young boy with obvious developmental differences who kept waving at us and hugging the women who lead the tour. They stood with pride next to the walls that had been stripped of graffiti. These activists had pushed back against the violent gangs. They had worked with local authorities and gang leaders to have their neighborhood declared a "peace zone." Both the Central American participants and the group from North America were impressed. Negotiating with local authorities and gangs wasn't easy work. The women had organized and had stood up for their rights. It was inspiring to hear them tell the story.

A year and a half later we heard reports from that community. An elite team of Salvadoran police, trained by the United States military, had come to the neighborhood. The leaders explained that this group, under pressure to show public results, had taken advantage of the neighborhood's bad reputation. They had accused local young men of gang activity and arrived to arrest them. The developmentally delayed boy was killed in the confrontation. A picture of his dead body was published on police social media, a semi-automatic weapon in his hand. The caption read, "Another rat is dead." The community leaders will tell anyone willing to listen that the photo must have been staged by the police. No one who knew the boy would have allowed him to hold a gun. He was barely verbal. There was no way he could have been actively involved in a firefight with police.

Cristosal's attorneys are looking into the case. It is unlikely the lawyers will be able to secure a settlement for the family and the community, like attorneys for Michael Brown's family secured from the city of Ferguson.[12] This case may prove difficult. Still, Cristosal takes on difficult cases.

David Morales, the director of Cristosal's legal program, describes the choices the team makes as "strategic litigation." Morales and his team look for emblematic cases, and they push for judicial rulings that help recognize a broader framework of rights. One case in particular has become the center of their efforts. As part of the peace accords in the 1990s, El Salvador's government granted "blanket amnesty." No crimes committed during the war could be prosecuted. But in recent years, courts have reversed the law and ruled that mass murder cases may be tried.

At Cristosal, Morales is leading the legal strategy to advance the case for the village of El Mozote.[13] In 1981, the second year of the civil war that followed Romero's death, Salvadoran forces murdered over eight hundred villagers—men, women, and children—in the rural town of Mozote. The massacre is the worst in

---

12 Kathie Goldgeier, "Michael Brown's Parents Settle Wrongful Death Lawsuit with Ferguson, MO," NPR, June 20, 2017, https://www.npr.org/sections/thetwo-way/2017/06/20/533738274/michael-browns-parents-settle-wrongful-death-lawsuit-with-ferguson-mo.

13 Robert Lowes, "'Activate' Citizens to Claim Human Rights, and Governments to Ensure Them, Say Cristosal Leaders," Episcopal News, October 11, 2018, https://www.episcopalnewsservice.org/2018//11/activate-citizens-to-claim-human-rights-and-governments-to-ensure-them-say-cristosal-leaders/.

the modern history of the Western Hemisphere. Cristosal's work on this case has brought international attention because a decision could set new legal precedent. If the military figures who ordered the massacre are brought to justice, it could set a framework for prosecuting police officers who commit extrajudicial killings today. A win could end impunity for military and police officers who kill Salvadorans.

When I take groups to El Salvador from St. Louis, we often start with questions about whether the trip will be safe. We come back to the United States with questions about how we might be involved in the kind of concrete work Cristosal is doing in our own courts and with our own elected representatives. We come back with a new perspective on whether El Salvador is a safe place, whether our own neighborhoods are really "peaceful." We come back hungry for more prophetic revolution.

5 ▪ *Building Peace with Myself*

Spiritual teachers often talk about the importance of "finding peace within yourself" before working for peace in your community. I think I always imagined this "inner peace" as a sort of blissful calm. If I do my meditation in the morning, I have a chance of being cool and collected when I approach work for peace during the day. The people with whom I work would be impressed. (How much spiritual work do we do to impress the folks around us?) I longed to be perceived this way. My inner calm could convey some sense of authority. Somewhere in my subconscious, as I meditated or prayed, I hoped that I could just conjure this postmeditation appearance. The appearance would give me credit as I tried to work for peace.

For much of my life I imagined that inner peace as an absence, a lack. If I could just have fewer appointments. If we could all just winnow down the number of activities to which we have to shuttle kids and family members. If I could just leave work a little earlier, have a little less in my life, I could find peace. Editing is never a bad idea, but I have found I can't subtract my way to peace.

Such a vision of peace can become problematic, especially for folks committed to justice work. While carefully editing commitments, and learning to practice saying "No" is important, this idea of a negative peace, a calm that could be found only be letting go of obligations, can be an impossible fiction. Changing unjust structures requires commitment; it requires time. Working for peace means showing up after work, after school, at community meetings, and cultivating relationships outside our usual social circles. Peace requires active commitment to building relationships, and building relationships is work.

Taking guidance from teachers like Dr. King and Archbishop Romero, I've come to believe in a peace that can't be found through subtraction. A peace that is the presence of justice requires a willingness to upset the status quo. If it is true in the streets, if it is true in the courts, if it is true in city hall, why wouldn't it be true for my own soul? Peace within myself doesn't come just because I quiet down my life.

St. Louis has invited me to a different sort of work for inner peace. The Ferguson uprising problematized not only my sense of "officers of the peace," but also my mindset about inner peace as well. In some meetings my practiced calm was questioned. Why wasn't I reacting? I heard activists say time and again, "Silence is violence." In Ferguson, a cool emotional state wasn't always a resource; it could be a liability. As a white person, my sitting quietly in the back of a room could be read as disengagement.

My presence was also complicated in Ferguson because I am ordained. My colleague the Rev. Willis Johnson is a Black United Methodist pastor. The *Washington Post* published a photo of him standing between a visibly angry young man and the police. The photo went viral, in part because it told a story that was true on the streets. Clergy are sometimes perceived by activists as being in the way, or as inappropriately trying to mediate or take the spotlight. While marches often start or end in churches, church leaders are not consistently trusted by organizers.

As a gay white ordained man, engagement in St. Louis's demonstrations around race equity can be difficult. If I push my way to the front of a line at a protest, or if I step in front of a television camera to answer questions, I could be overstepping. In Ferguson I had to learn to be more careful—to hear how my race, my gender, my ordination, and my age all spoke before I opened my mouth. If I showed up to a protest with a collar on and a reporter approached me, I learned to point them to one of the young leaders at the front of the action. I had to work to decenter my desire to be at the center, my desire to project a calm presence and make meaning of it all.

Engaging in cross-cultural multiracial work for peace and justice requires a different sort of inner peace that is less peace *within* yourself and more peace *with* yourself. This peace requires knowing my context, as well as knowing my identities and their intersections. This peace means knowing more about the historical structures of privilege with which I intersect. Finding peace with myself has meant returning to the stories that shaped me and asking about my perception of truths. This isn't the calm that comes because the storm has ceased, rather it is a comfort that happens as I get more comfortable riding the waves.

True inner peace doesn't ask me to disengage my feelings but rather to interrogate them. When I find myself feeling frustrated, inadequate, or entitled, I have learned to ask, "How do I think this meeting should be going? How do I imagine folks should be hearing me? Why do I think my preferred outcome should be the case?" Looking for this peace requires examining my own inner "shoulds," and asking what they say about me.

As a white person, this intentional work on identity doesn't come naturally. I have grown up with the privilege of being "normed." In classrooms and meetings, I was used to being heard. My ideas were valued in the spaces I was most comfortable occupying.

Around Ferguson, as I shared my perspective or an idea in meetings, I sometimes noticed the body language of the organizers shifted. There was caution, sometimes even hostility, when I took up space. When I asked a question or offered a suggestion too quickly, it was hard to face this feeling of being watched, and sometimes judged, before I spoke. Learning to strike a balance between engagement and not dominating the space has become an ongoing project for me.

Beginnings of This Work in My Story

In the years since the Ferguson uprising, I have found myself reflecting often on my sophomore year in college. The University of San Diego was founded in 1949. Fifty-three years later, the college elected its first Black student body president, Christopher Wilson. I was close friends with the newly elected vice president, Aisha Taylor, and she offered me one of forty or so student-government jobs. I was tapped to serve as director of social issues, organizing speakers and events for the student body around justice.

Early in the school year, the whole student government went on a long weekend retreat together, which also included leaders from the United Front Multicultural Center and Greek Life, the sorority and fraternity alliance. Historically, the Fall Leaders Retreat had been used to build relationships between those who planned the bulk of the college's student programming, to compare calendars and find ways not to conflict, and perhaps to collaborate on events. The agenda with the new administration was different. We were engaging in antiracism and bias-consciousness training, which involved a lot of storytelling.

Building Peace with Myself

That year of college I made the decision to come out publicly as gay. Though we were a progressive campus, at least for a Catholic school, it made me one of a handful of openly queer folks on the retreat. I had been in the process of coming out to myself for several years, and it had not been easy. I was in high school when Matthew Shepard was murdered, the victim of an antigay hate crime. Shepard was brutally beaten by two men who had pretended to be flirting with him at a bar in Laramie, Wyoming. They left him tied to a fencepost. He was found the next morning and rushed to a Fort Collins hospital. He died six days later, and his death became national news. All this occurred just a few hours from my childhood home. One of my mother's seminary professors preached at the largest public memorial service for the young man, which was held at St. John's Cathedral in Denver. As I was coming to terms with my own sexual orientation, I was faced with stories that told me naming my identity could be dangerous.

At the training retreat with my fellow student leaders, I talked about the fear for the first time publicly. I talked about Matthew Shepherd. I talked about the bullying I had faced growing up for my perceived orientation, even before I named it for myself. I cried in front of a hundred or so of my classmates. I was greeted with hugs and understanding tears. I was greeted with acceptance and solidarity. Then I heard more stories.

One of the leaders of the Black student organization stood up to talk about James Byrd. She said Byrd, a Black man, had accepted a ride home from a neighbor in Jasper, Texas. James didn't know it, but the neighbor was a white supremacist, and he didn't drive Byrd home. Instead the white man and two friends tied a rope around him and dragged him behind their truck until he died. His mutilated corpse was left on the front lawn of a historic Black church in the town. Byrd was murdered four months before Shepard, she said. I hadn't heard the story until she told it.

I was struck by the similarity and the difference in the fear she shared. Her fear didn't come with the question, "Can they tell?" Her identity was constantly visible in a way my orientation was not. Her fear was also generational. She shared the fear with parents, grandparents, and great grandparents. Every generation in her family had had to form their own responses to the threats and indignities of racism.

I listened as other students described fears that were less dramatic but still constant. Several people of color spoke of the fear that their white classmates would discount their opinions, that professors would read their papers with more scrutiny, that security officers would follow them through a mall, a neighborhood, or even on campus. At the heart of the stories was the subtle question, "What are you doing here?" It followed people of color wherever they went. It told them that their classroom, their neighborhood, even their dorm wasn't really made for them. Up until that night, I had often talked about why the University of San Diego had been a "perfect fit" for me. To a degree I was right, but in a way that was suddenly uncomfortable.

In the quiet that followed the storytelling, a disquiet grew within me. Growing up in a majority white Denver suburb, race was mostly treated as a joke. We made fun of a friend's immigrant parents for their strict rules. We laughed at accents. We pointed out that the only family of African Americans at our school seemed to supply a large number of the star basketball players. We didn't think of ourselves as "racist." These were only jokes. But subconsciously I had learned another set of behaviors.

I came to realize race had played a bigger role in how I moved through the world than I had been taught to acknowledge. I had already worked with the student government for a couple of months, and I remembered a meeting when I had discounted something our newly elected president had said. I had waited until my friend, the vice president, a white woman, repeated his idea and reinforced that it was the direction we were moving. I needed the repetition because subconsciously I was ignoring the input of a Black man. Racism was part of how I had learned to interact in the world.

I hadn't been raised a violent white supremacist, but I had learned subtly to whom I was supposed to listen. I had also learned to lock the doors of my car if I drove up to a corner and a group of Black men were standing on the sidewalk. On some level, I had always known this. I made judgements, sometimes consciously, but more often unconsciously based on race. Again, where I grew up, we didn't talk about race. Race was a joke, but we weren't "racists." We were clear on that. Sure, there was sometimes an undercurrent of fear that the growing Mexican population was coming to "steal our jobs," but that too was mostly talked about as a joke. I realized that not talking about race was itself a privilege of my so-called peaceful suburban upbringing.

I hadn't ever before listened to a group of my colleagues talk about how race had a direct impact in their lives. I found myself feeling guilty. Later in the retreat, I tried to confess to Christopher what I had realized. He didn't brush me off immediately. He patiently listened to my apology, but he also laughed, as if to say,

How Can I Live Peacefully with Justice?

"Do you not realize that I face this stuff every day?" He said essentially, "It's okay. Try not to do it again." My personal revelation wasn't going to be greeted as some world-changing epiphany either.

For a while, I was pretty earnest about this work. I came home to Colorado that Christmas, ready to share my newfound knowledge. My family often watched the movie *A Christmas Story* together. I always loved the scene where Ralphie has to wear a bunny suit on Christmas morning. But that year I interrupted the final scene when the family has Christmas dinner in a Chinese restaurant. I chastised my siblings for laughing at the accents of the waiters. My sister rolled her eyes at me. It took me awhile to realize I wasn't going to convert my family, my community, all at once. Our racist structures and biased ways of being took generations to build. They wouldn't be overcome by one college sophomore over one Christmas break.

That retreat, particularly the night of sharing stories, is a touchstone in my understanding of inner peace. Never before had I told such a large group about my sexual orientation. Never before had I shared my fear with a group that listened so intently. My story was met with embrace. And that mattered to me more than I knew it could. I felt safer because I was accepted and heard. I felt more whole.

The embrace also complicated my life because, in part, that embrace came with a trust. I had been trusted with some of the fear and frustration that my neighbors faced every day. Vulnerability was met with vulnerability. And I knew that honoring the stories that were shared with me would require me to keep working. Peace-building meant committing to my own inner work and to outward work in my community for equity.

A Theological Framework for Inner Peace

In the months that followed, I tried to notice how often race, gender, age, class, language, and other social dynamics played into what I heard or in what I questioned in a classroom dynamic or a meeting. I also started to read more theologians of color. I had come to the University of San Diego with an agenda to study theology. And I came to college expecting to learn about a particular set of theologians, almost all of them white European men.

When Archbishop Demond Tutu talks of the Christian value of diversity and our intrinsic interconnection as children of God, he speaks of the value of *ubuntu*.[14] The word comes from the Xhosa people of South Africa. In contrast to the Western European philosophical tradition—Decartes's "I think therefore I am"—Tutu says, *ubuntu* sources identity in the other. "I am because you are," Tutu teaches. Without you, I cannot be. If you are not fully yourself, I cannot be fully myself.

If my wholeness depends on your wholeness, I cannot be fully myself if you cannot be fully yourself. A world that privileges me also robs me. When I am privileged, I am also robbed of the full contribution, the full humanity, of my neighbor. When I have been trusted with someone's story, when I have been counted as an ally, something opens in the relationship, something deepens. When the wounds that I often shield from the light of day, from the scrutiny of others, have been honestly heard, I experience a freedom. The moments are fleeting, but they are enough to keep me walking. Real peace-building comes in relationship.

---

14 Desmond Tutu, *No Future Without Forgiveness* (New York: Doubleday, 1999), 31.

How Can I Live Peacefully with Justice?

I knew about living as less than my full self. I knew about hiding identity. As a queer teenager, I had learned to minimize behaviors that could be read as "gay." I had learned to be quiet in certain conversations about dating and sex. I knew that if others knew me fully, I might not be understood. I might not be accepted. I might be in danger. Coming to peace with myself wasn't always peaceful. Sometimes it meant taking risks.

That sophomore year, I heard stories I'd never heard before, about how difficult it was for a Black man or a Latina woman to navigate a space designed by and for white students. I heard so many stories about folks who chose to be quiet, not to contribute, because they didn't want to lose a place at the school, or lose a job. They didn't want to be labeled a problem. They didn't want to risk a scholarship or simply be labeled as an "angry Black" person. The path to success was to keep your head down and avoid notice.

In that second year of college, I learned about ways colleagues and friends were also hiding. I had come from a predominantly white high school to a predominantly white college. When I accepted the admission, I honestly thought that my university was diverse. Only 20 percent of the student body were people of color. I have learned since that white folks tend to overestimate the diversity of a room. White folks who go to a church where some people of color worship will say their church is half white and half non-white. Actively listening to the voices of people who are marginalized because of race, gender, ethnicity, immigrant status, age or ability takes more commitment than looking for visible diversity on brochures. It means opening yourself and your institution up for change.

Latin American liberation theologians often talk about the communion table as a "foretaste" of God's reign.[15] In the Eucharist we glimpse what life will be like when we are all gathered together by Christ's love. I have come to believe that in order for God's reign to arrive, the systems of discrimination we have inherited and reinforced must be dismantled. I am grateful to serve in a church that is visibly diverse, but the sense of communion deepens when I know more about the lives of the folks with whom I break bread. I have only glimpsed a sense of the relationships that could be possible. The moments of breakthrough have been just that, moments.

Theologian Willie Jennings has written of these moments of encounter, of communion across difference that "it is precisely the episodic character of this capacity among Christians that indicates something deeply, painfully amiss."[16] When we get a taste of what is possible, when we are trusted with one another's stories and one another's pain, the experience is one of blessed trust. And it is true that glimpsing the world as it should be forces us to wrestle with the world as it is. When we catch momentary sight of the peace we seek, we also see how far we have to go.

Practicality, Whiteness, and Letting Go of Quick Fixes

After college as I said, I served for two years as a lay chaplain for the Episcopal Church at the University of California, San Diego

---

15 Victor Cordina, "Sacraments," in *Systematic Theology: Perspectives from Liberation Theology,* ed. Jon Sobrino and Ignacio Ellacuría (New York: Orbis Books, 2003). pp. 221-223.

16 Willie Jennings, *The Christian Imagination: Theology and the Origins of Race* (New Haven: Yale University Press, 2010),13.

(UCSD). I was graciously invited to participate in programming by the LGBT Resource Center on that campus. Even with my own propensity to overestimate diversity, the LGBT center at UCSD was a remarkably interracial and intercultural space.

At UCSD there was norm that was often introduced in group processes: "step up / step back." A facilitator would explain that all of us, because of our subconscious experience of bias and privilege, and also because of our own propensity for extroversion or introversion, have work to do in group settings. People who are prone to talk, to process out loud, to share their opinions, need to work to "step back" if a group is going to function well, to make room for others. Those whose input has not been historically valued, or who have a fear of sharing, need to "step up." I knew that far more often than not, my work in a group was the work of stepping back. It was up to me to learn to listen. As I engaged in Ferguson. I often found the need to say to myself, "Step back," before opening my mouth and offering a proposed solution. If I didn't catch myself in time, I saw the raised eyebrows of activists.

The stories that were trusted to me in college also helped me to know that in 2014, something radical was happening in St. Louis. The stories I had heard, the fear that was named only in spaces where people of color felt semisafe, a part of that hidden story was being shared for the world to see. Black folks in my city were done being quiet. Black mothers were sick of worrying about whether their child would make it home safely. Black parents were sick of teaching their children how to behave in front of police officers, so they wouldn't get shot. People were done keeping their pain private. The Black community was telling the story, was letting the anger show.

It took a lot of inner peace-building for me to come to meetings in Ferguson without a list of solutions. I had a sense that activists would have shouted down many of my solutions, quick fixes I wanted to offer. I had watched this happen to other white folks. Still, my gut response to the unrest was to try and solve the problem. Showing up not for the sake of fixing, but just for the sake of showing up was hard. Prayer and meditation helped. But the work wasn't about finding peace "within" myself as much as peace "with" myself, with my identity. I needed to let go of my need to be part of a quick fix.

Making Peace with Myself for the Sake of Pursuing Justice beyond Myself

White kids are often told they can find a solution. White kids, like me, are taught that they can find an answer. This system of reward creates a desire to solve problems. Internally, I know, I still want to get a sticker for my response. Stickers aren't going to save us. A lot of my peacemaking work internally is about making peace with not always being able to solve problems. Building peace within myself is about letting go of my cultivated inner need to get it right.

I share these reflections on inner peace not because I think I have reached an enlightened state, but because I am still navigating. There are times I know I still keep quiet because I worry my openly queer self would not be safe, would not be welcome. And there are times I know that my learned desire to be rewarded for my perspective, for having the right answer, gets me in trouble for offering an idea with too much zeal. I still often take up too much space in a class discussion or a meeting.

How Can I Live Peacefully with Justice?

I don't think inner peace with who I am and how I am perceived will come like a calm after the storm. But at times, I find myself enjoying the ride on the waves. I know that when I am comfortable in my own skin, when I have a sense how I might be read because of that skin, or because of the sound of my voice, or the gender of my spouse, I can be more effective in my work for justice and peace.

I have learned that building real and lasting peace isn't about coming to correct answers quickly. The work is generational. It's about building systems of equity to replace systems of inequity. Structural injustice took hundreds of years to build and rebuild. It shouldn't surprise me that we won't solve it in one meeting. I've also noticed how much more often my white friends talk about longing for peace. People of color in my life talk more about justice. This may be anecdotal. It may also reflect a wider trend.

Peace has been defined for generations by white folks, by men, by people in power. If we want to know a different kind of peace, more folks will be needed to help write the definition. If we want to know real peace, we'll have to know how we have perpetuated and benefited from deeply racist systems of policing and power. We will have to know justice.

Epilogue

This book was long delayed, which means that these last words are being written as we again face a season of uncovering. In the early days of the pandemic, the coronavirus was labeled a great "equalizer."[17] As the weeks wore on, the virus instead exposed great inequality. The virus was infecting and killing African American and Latino communities at a far higher rate than in white neighborhoods. The virus has exposed injustices publicly that have been long been fostered in our communities.

Then, two-and-a-half months into the coronavirus shutdown, I was once again in the streets hearing the chant, "No justice, no peace, no racist police." More names were added to those of Michael Brown, Tamir Rice, Sandra Bland, and Eric Garner. Breonna Taylor, Ahmaud Arbery, and George Floyd's deaths uncovered how little has changed in the past six years. I watched as a fire was set in the basement of St. John's, my former parish, and as the President tried to use the church for his political gain. I was proud to see my former parish stand up, and to hear Bishop Mariann Budde call our nation not to be distracted by a building, but to keep our focus on racial injustice. I spoke with clergy friends around the country. We compared notes on protests in Ferguson, Minneapolis, and Lafayette Square. There are still so many hearts that need to open, so many secrets to be unhidden.

---

17 "Gov. Cuomo Is Wrong: Covid-19 Is Anything but an Equalizer," Washington Post, April 5, 2020, https://www.washingtonpost.com/outlook/2020/04/05/gov-cuomo-is-wrong-covid-19-is-anything-an-equalizer/.

How Can I Live Peacefully with Justice?

We have a choice in the months ahead. We can work for a "return" in the same way that so many white leaders in St. Louis fought for a return to the "peaceful" days before Ferguson, or we can choose to keep looking to the root causes. We can keep our eyes not on the way things were, but on the road ahead. We can move forward to a more equitable future. The work will be slower than we would like.

As Christians we have companions in the journey. Jesus taught a way of self-offering love for neighbor, a way that lead to a very different vision of peace. Modern saints like Dr. King and Oscar Romero have pointed us back to that way, challenged us not to define peace negatively as the "absence of conflict" but rather as the "presence of justice." As Christians today, we also have the privilege of witnessing a potentially revolutionary moment. Communities that have long suffered injustice are claiming their human rights through protest, through advocacy. As followers of Jesus, we have to ask ourselves, will we show up?

Justice work can make you tired. Work for peace can wear you down. It's not comfortable work, because pursuing true peace asks you to give up your assumptions. Working for justice asks you to give up a desire to "return to normal."

For a priest in St. Louis, perhaps Jeremiah names the tension I feel around the word "peace" the best. Faced with invasion and exile, the prophet looks to the root causes of Israel's suffering: "Everyone is greedy for unjust gain; and from prophet to priest, everyone deals falsely. They have treated the wound of my people carelessly, saying, 'Peace, peace', when there is no peace."(Jeremiah 6:13b-14). If we want to live with peace, we will have to first let go of the unjust "peace" for which we have settled. We will have to allow for uncovering and work to build relationships of trust. We will have to learn not to treat wounds carelessly.

www.ingramcontent.com/pod-product-compliance
Lightning Source LLC
Chambersburg PA
CBHW070857050426
42453CB00012B/2249